Forgiveness:
making sense of it

John Phillips

Forgiveness:
making sense of it

Contents

Making Sense Of Forgiveness

To forgive is a choice which we all have to face. In the course of our daily lives people hurt us. We also share the pain when a family member or close friend is hurt.

Unforgiveness is a major issue for our society. An unwillingness to forgive lies at the heart of so much conflict within, and between, families and communities.

It was the recognition of this issue that prompted HMP/YOI Downview to establish its Seeds of Forgiveness project in June 2009, for which a short booklet was produced.

The purpose in reproducing that booklet has been two-fold; firstly, to include a brief outline of what the Bible teaches on forgiveness, especially of our need of God's forgiveness and, secondly, to make the booklet available more widely.

If it helps some to begin their own journey towards forgiveness, whether to grant it or receive it, I will have achieved my objective. Certainly, all who read it will be inspired by the moving stories of forgiveness by people whose lives have been torn apart by acts of extreme violence.

I particularly wish to thank Rev. Rosie Deedes (Anglican Chaplain, HMP Isle of Wight, Albany Site), who championed Seeds of Forgiveness whilst chaplain at HMP/YOI Downview, deeply committed as she is to see people set free from hatred, anger and bitterness, the hallmarks of unforgiveness.

Too many people have helped with this booklet to enable me to mention them by name. They know who they are! They also know how much I have appreciated their input!

John Phillips
March 2010

Part One:

Forgiveness - making sense of it

What is forgiveness?

To forgive is to give up:

- any feelings of bitterness and resentment towards a person who has hurt us
- any desire for revenge or any desire to harm the person.

It is important to understand what forgiveness does not involve. To forgive does *not* mean that we:

- pretend the incident didn't happen
- trivialise the hurt
- make excuses for what happened
- ignore the need for justice
- must continue any relationship with the person.

So, forgiveness does not override the need for justice where a criminal offence has been committed and it does not mean that there should not be compensation, for personal injury, for example. However, when you forgive you do not hate the person who hurt you and you do not desire revenge.

The practice of forgiveness is our most important
contribution to the healing of the world.
Marianne Williamson

Diane's Story

Diane Nichols has had an amazing journey to forgiveness from a quite awful tragedy. Her husband murdered the 19-year-old girl with whom he was having an affair.

His imprisonment led Diane, ultimately, into an emotional prison of her own. Eventually, she reached the point of knowing that she had to forgive her husband. She confronted him with the devastating pain he had caused her and their children. "What you did really hurt us but it hurts even more to hate you for it. We want to forgive you."

Forgiving her husband removed that extra pain and brought a measure of healing for Diane. She explained: "I never thought I could feel this way or come to a place of forgiving but it's what I needed to do. I was literally dying inside ... forgiving was the way to heal."

> What you did really hurt us but it hurts even more to hate you for it...
>
> I was literally dying inside... forgiving was the way to heal.

From A Prison of My Own courtesy of David C. Cook.

Harbouring unforgiveness is like drinking poison and hoping the other person will die!

Forgive and forget?

No! Forgiving a serious wrong can be incredibly difficult and may take time; forgetting it may never happen.

However, when we forgive we will not wish to dwell upon the past and the pain will lessen with time. On the other hand, if we refuse to forgive, the healing process cannot take place. Then, the harbouring of resentment and bitterness will cause us to constantly re-live the horror of the event.

Why should we forgive?

We might think that refusing to forgive people is our one lawful option of making them pay for what they have done. It helps us to feel that we are in control and we haven't let them off the hook. It is our way of trying to hurt them.

However, do we really achieve that? Sometimes we may. We may make it more difficult for them to move on with their life. But, often, their own sense of guilt and shame will be their real stumbling block - their inability to forgive themselves.

It is important to realise that the person who is always affected by unforgiveness is the victim. It has been said: "Harbouring unforgiveness is like drinking poison and hoping the other person will die!"

How true that is. Poisoning ourselves is exactly what we do when we choose not to forgive. Our anger may not have any impact at all upon the other person; indeed, they may not even be aware of it. Then, not only do we fail to get the victim to drink the poison but we take it ourselves.

How do we forgive?

Forgiveness can take time.

The way in which a person forgives and the time over which it happens will normally depend upon the seriousness of the offence and what remorse has been shown.

Most of us, most of the time, will try to brush off minor hurts which are a part of life. We forgive the person.

However, when something serious happens, we can react quite differently. To contemplate forgiving the person may be even more difficult if it is a family member or close friend who has been hurt.

As we have seen, the way we react can affect ourselves even more than those who are to blame.

From time to time, we read of a victim of a serious crime who, within days or even hours, is explaining that they forgive the person responsible. Very few people are able to respond in that way. Most are unable to think beyond their initial anger and they need to take time to reflect on how they truly feel towards the offender.

Ruth's Story

As a child, Ruth was raped by a family member over a period of several years.

"I have been on a journey for much of my life, looking to find peace. For me this road is about reconciliation and choice. I have a yearning, a calling towards peace. And hatred towards another or towards myself is not going to lead me towards peace. I have had to learn to forgive myself for not telling anyone, for not saying 'no', for not getting help. I have had to learn not to hate myself.

As for the person who did this to me, I can honestly say that my overwhelming feeling is compassion. To wound someone like that can only be done by someone who hates themselves, who has no respect for themselves and who is suffering deeply.

At times my fear and anger towards him and myself has been

8

overwhelming. I have battled with self-harm, suicidal yearnings, self-loathing and still now I have to actively choose to turn away from those mechanisms that I used to survive.

The biggest turning point has been realising I have a choice in hcw I respond to how I feel. I do not have to indulge those feelings of loathing, self-hatred or powerlessness. I cannot change what happened to me but I can change my response to it.

So much of my life is now healed, I am happily married with children. So much is happy and my face is, mostly, tipped up towards the sun. The bits that are still sore I am learning to live alongside and find reconciliation with. I do not fight them any more but we are learning to live with each other.

I am learning over and over, as I did as a child, to choose life, to choose saying 'yes' and to choose to love. It has been so hard to get here, so hard to find a way to choose to live again but so worthwhile."

> The biggest turning point has been realising I have a choice in how I respond to how I feel.
>
> I cannot change what happened to me but I can change my response to it.

Courtesy of The Forgiveness Project: www.theforgivenessproject.com

---

He who is devoid of the power to forgive
is devoid of the power to love.
Martin Luther King Jr

Forgiveness is not a feeling

There will come a time when we will have to decide whether to forgive - and give up our anger and resentment - whatever our feelings might be.

If we choose to forgive, we may have to remind ourselves regularly of that decision, in order to avoid slipping back into the feelings of anger. Should we tell the person that we have forgiven them? It is best if we do. If they are feeling shame and guilt it will help them to know that they have been forgiven.

It can also help us, for we are then able to point to a specific time when we chose to forgive. If we do it face to face, it can be a good idea to write a letter as well and retain it as a record, and reminder, of what we have done.

Seeking support from others

There will be times when no one else is aware that we have been hurt. We may then feel a need to talk with someone and, perhaps, seek their advice. That can be an essential first step towards healing.

However, we must be very clear about our true motive for wishing to do so. Are we really looking for a 'listening ear' to unburden ourselves? Or is our main objective to make it known how badly the other person has behaved towards us? Is this our first step towards revenge, by damaging their reputation and hoping to cause others to think badly of them too?

It is often good to take time to reflect on whether it will be right to share it with others; if so, with whom and how much needs to be said.

- -

If we really want to love, we must learn how to forgive.
Mother Theresa

- -

When we have been hurt unwittingly

As people, we are sensitive and it is often the case that someone doesn't know that they have actually hurt us. Obviously, we can be hurt not only by what they do but also by what they say - and, equally, by what they don't do or don't say.

The need to choose whether to forgive still applies, coupled with the need to decide whether we should make them aware that they have offended us. There will be times when it will be right to do so, if only to reduce the risk that they will do the same thing again. At other times it will be best not to say anything, to avoid damaging the relationship.

Barry & Margaret's Story

In May 2008 Barry and Margaret Mizen's 16-year-old son, Jimmy, was attacked and killed at a baker's shop in South East London.

Their reaction to this horrendous crime has amazed their friends and the community.

"We have a faith and we believe in forgiveness. We have not had any sense of anger or any sense of a need for revenge.

We long for and pray for peace in the world and in our communities and we will not allow any anger to destroy the peace which we desire for our family.

Our friends have been surprised by our reaction and assured us that the anger will come but it hasn't. There has been plenty of pain, yes, and, at times, the pain has almost overwhelmed us.

But anger? No, and no desire for revenge. We could not cope with anger on top of the incredible pain which Jimmy's death has brought to our family."

> We could not cope with anger on top of the incredible pain which Jimmy's death has brought to our family.

Objections to forgiveness

'They don't deserve it.'

It is not uncommon to hear the excuse that the person doesn't deserve to be forgiven and that will often be true.

Sheree Osborne was abandoned by her mother and dreadfully abused by her father. As an adult, she was horrified when a friend told her that she needed to forgive her parents.

She recalls her response: " ...my heart hit the floor and I could feel a sickness rising up inside of me. Forgive them! Why should I? What right did they have to be let off the hook like that? I could feel the sickness turn to anger. I had hated them for so many years for what they had done to me. I was not about to forgive them now and say that it was all right for them to have done that – no way! ...If I forgive them it will be like they have won!"

Yet Sheree began to recognise that the advice she was being given was for her own benefit; she was the only one who was suffering.

Finally, through the support and encouragement of that friend, Sheree realised that she had to take that step to forgive, for her own sake. "I had a life to live and I wanted some quality within it. If this forgiveness was the price, then I would have to do it. So I chose to forgive."

'It's a sign of weakness.'

Often, those who say that forgiveness is a sign of weakness misunderstand what it actually means to forgive. It does not mean that we simply overlook or ignore the wrong. It recognises the wrong and it

----

The weak can never forgive.
Forgiveness is the attribute of the strong.
Mohandas (Mahatma) Gandhi

----

recognises the need for justice and punishment. However, it does not look for personal vengeance, through hatred or through any other means. The reality is you have to be very strong to forgive. To forgive a serious offence may be the toughest thing you ever do.

'It would be a betrayal.'

If a child has been hurt or killed, it can feel like betraying the child if the parents forgive. Mary Foley sensed that some of her friends had those thoughts:

Mary's Story

In 2005 Mary Foley's 15-year-old daughter, Charlotte, was murdered during a birthday party in East London. In February 2006 an 18-year-old girl was jailed for life for the unprovoked attack.

"Two weeks after Charlotte's death, God gave me the grace and strength to forgive. ... I knew that if I didn't forgive, anger and bitterness would turn me into a person Charlotte would not have liked, or my family and friends for that fact.

Some months after the trial, Charlotte's killer wrote to me saying she was very sorry and that she didn't mean to kill Charlotte. She said it had been a moment of madness. I was pleased to get the letter and wrote back telling her I'd forgiven her.

Some people tell me I'm brave and strong - but others don't say much. Although no one has come up to me and said: "You can't have loved your daughter to forgive her killer", I'm sure that's what they think at times, and I understand that, because some people are disgusted by the very idea of forgiveness. It can seem like an act of betrayal. But, on the contrary, it's an act of freedom."

> It can seem like an act of betrayal
> ...on the contrary, it's an act of freedom.

Courtesy of The Forgiveness Project: www.theforgivenessproject.com

Katy's Story

In 1997, Katy Hutchison's husband, Bob, was beaten to death while checking on a party being thrown by their neighbour's son in British Columbia.

A wall of silence meant that it was four years before Ryan admitted to having delivered the fatal blow.

Katy:
"That confession would begin the healing process for both of us. He then stunned police by asking to meet me. Within 24 hours of his arrest, I found myself face-to-face with the man who had murdered my husband.

As he sobbed it was all I could do not to hold him. Second to the day I gave birth, it was probably the most human moment of my life.

Forgiveness isn't easy. Taking tranquilizers and having someone look after your kids would probably be easier ...

Whether victim or perpetrator, part of being human is rolling up our sleeves and taking an active part in repairing harm... Forgiveness became an opportunity to create a new and hopeful beginning."

> Katy's forgiveness is the most incredible thing that anyone has ever given me. It changed my life.

Ryan:
"Katy's forgiveness is the most incredible thing that anyone has ever given me. My life would still be full of anger and violence if it wasn't for Katy.

Doing time is easy compared to the guilt I'll have to live with for the rest of my life. But with Katy's forgiveness, I hope that one day I'll be able to forgive myself."

> ...part of being human is rolling up our sleeves and taking an active part in repairing harm.

Courtesy of The Forgiveness Project: www.theforgivenessproject.com

'But he hasn't said sorry.'

When there is no apology and people don't seem sorry, it can be even more difficult to forgive. For Ray and Vi Donovan, they had to take the first step themselves.

In 2001 their son, Christopher, was murdered by a group of youths. Ray decided that he had to forgive their son's killers. Later, Vi was also able to do so. Following the conviction of those responsible, Ray and Vi wrote to one of the killers to tell him that they had forgiven him.

Ray explained: "Ryan needed to know that we had forgiven him. You shouldn't have to wait until the person says sorry. It is not the person who needs to say sorry that matters; it's you, humbling yourself and saying 'I forgive' that matters, whether they accept it or not."

'What's the point? Our relationship is over.'

To forgive someone we know does not necessarily mean that our relationship with that person has to continue. If there is a loss of trust, the relationship will certainly suffer, or may have to end, unless (and until) the trust can be rebuilt. To suggest that forgiveness and reconciliation must always go together is another misunderstanding about what it really means to forgive.

However, whatever happens, or whatever may be decided, concerning any relationship, forgiveness is still important for both parties. Without it, there will be continued resentment and no closure.

When a deep injury is done us,
we never recover until we forgive.
Alan Paton

Steven's Story

When police officer Steven McDonald entered Central Park, New York one afternoon in July 1986, he had no reason to think that his life would be threatened. However, a few minutes later a 15-year-old boy shot him in the head and in the throat at close range.

"The medical team did the impossible: they saved me, but my wounds were devastating. I was paralyzed from the neck down.

When the surgeon came to tell me this, my wife, Patti Ann, was there, and he told her I would need to be institutionalized. We had been married just eight months, and Patti Ann, who was 23, was three months pregnant. She collapsed to the floor, crying uncontrollably.

The birth of our baby boy, Conor, was like a message from God that I should live, and live differently. ...I prayed that I would be changed, that the person I was would be replaced by something new.

That prayer was answered with a desire to forgive Shavod, the young man who had shot me. I wanted to free myself of all the negative, destructive emotions that his act of violence had unleashed in me: anger, bitterness, hatred, and other feelings. I needed to do that so that I could love my wife and our child and those around us.

I believe the only thing worse than receiving a bullet in my spine would have been to nurture revenge in my heart. Such an attitude would have extended my injury to my soul, hurting others even more.

....when you forgive, you're always a winner. You don't lose a thing. It's not a sign of weakness to love somebody who hurts you. It's a sign of strength."

> ...the only thing worse than receiving a bullet in my spine would have been to nurture revenge in my heart.
>
> ...when you forgive, you're always a winner. You don't lose a thing.

From Why Forgive? courtesy of Plough Publishing House.

16

When we need others to forgive us

This look at forgiveness would not be complete without looking at the flipside of the coin - an acknowledgement of the fact that there are times when we are the offender rather than the victim.

We have all hurt other people by what we have done or said - and we will almost certainly find ourselves hurting people again in the future. Our first response should always be an acknowledgement of what we have done.

Saying sorry and making amends

It is really important to apologise and without making excuses. As Kimberley Johnson said, 'Never ruin an apology with an excuse.' The words 'I am sorry' are tremendously powerful. They can have an incredible impact upon a victim.

However, as Ray Donovan has said (see page 15), it is not good for a victim to hold back on forgiving a person until there is an apology, for one may never be forthcoming. At the same time, it is certainly true that for many people a genuine expression of remorse is just what is needed to help them to respond by forgiving.

It is also important for the offender to take whatever practical steps may be possible to make amends for the harm caused. That will reinforce the apology and will help to bring healing.

As Katy Hutchison has remarked (see page 14): 'Whether victim or perpetrator, part of being human is rolling up our sleeves and taking an active part in repairing harm.'

- -

Forgiveness does not change the past,
but it does enlarge the future.
Paul Boese

- -

Peter's Story

The damage done
"Today I am fifty-one and I have spent most of my life in and out of jail. For over thirty years heroin has been my best friend and my worst enemy. My liver was failing, my kidneys were shutting down and poison ran through my veins. But I didn't care whether I lived or died because I knew no one else did.

Then I met Will, a man who I'd attacked to get money for my next high. For some reason he chose to forgive me. Now I realise that I've only just begun to live."

> For some reason he chose to forgive me. Now I realise that I've only just begun to live.

Making amends
"Following my meeting with Will, I made promises about making amends to the anonymous victims of the thousands of crimes I had committed. But saying sorry to nameless, faceless people was going to be hard, if not impossible.

And so I decided that I would learn to help other people - people like me."

That is precisely what Peter is now doing. He is helping to turn prolific and priority offenders away from crime.

From *The Damage Done* courtesy of Bantam Press.

18

Forgive myself? Never!

It is very painful to see people's lives torn apart by unforgiveness. It is no different with those who are unable to forgive themselves.

Much of what has been said about forgiveness applies equally to forgiving oneself. It doesn't mean that we have to, or can, forget what we have done. It does mean acknowledging what has happened and then making the choice to forgive ourselves and release ourselves from the guilt, rather than allow self-hate to take hold.

Many people struggle to forgive themselves. Nevertheless, the reality is that whatever mistakes we might have made, whatever laws we might have broken and whatever damage and pain has resulted, we cannot change what has happened.

We are faced with two options. We can hate ourselves for what we have done, which will trap us in a life of pain and negativity, not only for ourselves but also for those whom we love.

The alternative is to receive forgiveness and move forward, using our time, energy and skills in ways that will truly be of positive benefit to others.

Peter, whose story is on page 18, was faced with exactly that choice. He chose to start making amends for the harm he had caused. That must always be the right choice.

Forgiveness can seem like an act of betrayal;
on the contrary, it's an act of freedom.
Mary Foley

Forgiveness

When the wind blows
And the sun shines
And the rainfall hits the ground;
When I breathe in
And I see things
I wish I could turn it around.

I can't earn it
Don't deserve it
It won't take away the pain;
I'm not worthy
Have no power
And I wouldn't do it again.

I can't ask for you to give me
The things I need to move at last,
Away from all the misery and hurt
That trail forward from my past.

Whatever things need doing
I would gladly play my part,
If only you could find for me
Forgiveness in your heart.

If I could only change the world
The first thing I would do,
Is make me in a different way
So I'd never have hurt you
- forgive me.

by VH

*From Seeds of Forgiveness - Poems by Prisoners in HMP Downview,
courtesy of BAR NONE Books.*

Part Two:

Forgiveness - how the Bible sees it

Ray and Vi Donovan are Christians and try to live according to the Bible's teaching. Their faith played a big part in their decision to forgive their son's killer (page 15). That was also true for Barry and Margaret Mizen (page 11).

Part Two of this booklet gives a brief outline of some of the important things the Bible has to say about forgiveness, both in regard to forgiving others and crucially, our need of God's forgiveness.

The most well known words about forgiveness are those in the Lord's Prayer, which Jesus taught His disciples as a 'model' prayer.

Forgive us our debts, as we also have forgiven our debtors.
Matthew 6:12

We will consider firstly, the request to God that He forgives us and secondly, the fact that God expects us to forgive others.

'Forgive us our debts...'

As we think about this request for God's forgiveness, there are two questions which really need to be answered:

- why do we need God's forgiveness?
- how do we receive God's forgiveness?

First, it is important to understand what Jesus meant by the word 'debt'. The Lord's Prayer is also recorded in Luke's Gospel chapter 11 and in that passage, the word 'sin' is used. We owe a 'debt' to God for every 'sin' we commit. We sin whenever we break one of God's laws or commandments.

Our debtors, as we shall see later, are those who have offended us in some way: they owe us a debt.

Our need of God's forgiveness

The Bible tells us that God created us in His own image and that we should love Him more than anyone or anything else.

So God created man in his own image, in the image of God he created him.

Genesis 1:27

Jesus replied: "'Love the Lord your God with all your heart and with all your soul and with all your mind.' This is the first and greatest commandment..."

Matthew 22:37,38

However, the Bible makes it clear that every person who has ever lived has failed to meet God's standard of absolute purity and holiness.

...for all have sinned and fall short of the glory of God...
Romans 3:23

Our sins prevent us from having that relationship with God for which we were created and which He longs to have with each of us: we are in debt to God as the Lord's Prayer puts it.

Whilst many people acknowledge that, they reason that God is full of love, compassion and mercy and is just longing to forgive us. Surely, they conclude, all that we need to do is ask God to forgive us. He will be satisfied and will forgive us.

It is certainly true that God does love us and is compassionate and merciful. However, He is a God of justice too. Being just means that He cannot simply overlook our sins: there has to be a punishment. How then, can God forgive us without punishing us?

The way to God's forgiveness

There was only one way in which God was able to satisfy His desire to be merciful to us and, at the same time, satisfy His need for justice. It required someone to take the punishment on our behalf. It required someone who Himself was not guilty of any sin against God: someone who was not in debt to God. There was just one person able to do that: Jesus, God's Son.

> *For God so loved the world that he gave his one and only Son, that whoever believes in him shall not perish but have eternal life.*
>
> John 3:16

Jesus took the punishment for our sins as He was crucified.

> *He himself bore our sins in his body on the tree, so that we might die to sins and live for righteousness; by his wounds you have been healed*
>
> 1 Peter 2:24

> *In him we have redemption through his blood, the forgiveness of sins, in accordance with the riches of God's grace.*
>
> Ephesians 1:7

God sent Jesus to pay our debts for us. However, we have to choose whether to accept that gift of forgiveness. We must understand that it is a gift. It is not a reward that we can ever merit.

> *For it is by grace you have been saved, through faith - and this not from yourselves, it is the gift of God - not by works, so that no-one can boast.*
>
> Ephesians 2:8,9

This is bad news for those who follow the popular belief that God will judge us - and reward us - according to our 'good works'. The idea that we can earn God's acceptance may be a widely held view but it is not what the Bible teaches.

Jesus illustrated this with a parable about a Pharisee and a tax collector. The Pharisees were known for their strict observance of the Old Testament laws, going far beyond what the law intended. This led to their self-righteousness and pride and to their own belief that they were the 'pillars of society'.

Jesus contrasted them with the tax collectors, who were despised by their fellow Jews for two reasons. Firstly, they were employed by the Romans and therefore viewed as traitors and secondly, they charged a little extra (or even more than a little) for their own pockets.

Two men went up to the temple to pray, one a Pharisee and the other a tax collector.

The Pharisee stood up and prayed about himself: 'God, I thank you that I am not like other men - robbers, evildoers, adulterers - or even like this tax collector. I fast twice a week and give a tenth of all I get.'

But the tax collector stood at a distance. He would not even look up to heaven, but beat his breast and said, 'God, have mercy on me, a sinner.'

Luke 18:10-14

Jesus explained that it was the tax collector's attitude that pleased God. He was the one who received what he asked for – God's mercy. The Pharisee failed to ask for God's mercy, for he failed to see that he needed it; foolishly, he was confident in his own righteousness.

This is wonderful news for today's 'tax collectors': those who feel that they have 'messed up' so much that God Himself must despise them, as well as society. It is wonderful news for those who feel that there is no way back.

There is a way back to God - but only one way. That one way is Jesus Himself. Jesus said:

> *I am the way and the truth and the life. No-one comes to the Father except through me.*
>
> John 14:6

The way of forgiveness and reconciliation which God has opened up for us may seem so simple. Yet it is so hard for 'religious' people who believe that their religious practices or their 'good works' will be sufficient to earn their entry permit to heaven. It is so hard for the proud who feel that they must, and can, earn God's forgiveness and acceptance.

It is only by God's grace that we can receive His forgiveness; it can never be ours by merit. He gave Jesus as the sacrifice for our sins and longs that we would accept Jesus as the way back to the Father.

Living with God's forgiveness

So, if we do receive God's forgiveness, what practical difference does it make to our lives? When we receive Jesus Christ as our 'saviour', recognising that He suffered our punishment, the Bible speaks of us as being 'in Christ'. It is like making a brand new start with Jesus at the centre of our life.

> *Therefore, if anyone is in Christ, he is a new creation; the old has gone, the new has come!*
>
> 2 Corinthians 5:17

This does not mean that we suddenly become perfect! Nor does it mean that all our problems and struggles suddenly disappear.

However, it *does* mean that we will have God's power working in us - the Holy Spirit - to help us overcome the continuing temptations which we face. It does mean that the Holy Spirit will be our helper to live in a way that is pleasing to God.

And it does mean, of course, that we have the great joy of knowing that Jesus Christ has paid the debt for us: that we will not receive the punishment we deserve when the day of judgment comes.

Living without God's forgiveness

The alternative to receiving God's forgiveness - the only other option - is to face God's wrath and punishment ourselves.

It is important that we truly understand the consequence of that choice. The Bible speaks very harshly of those who choose not to receive God's mercy and kindness.

Or do you show contempt for the riches of his kindness, tolerance and patience, not realising that God's kindness leads you towards repentance?

But because of your stubbornness and your unrepentant heart, you are storing up wrath against yourself for the day of God's wrath, when his righteous judgment will be revealed.

Romans 2:4,5

The Bible tells us that Jesus Himself, who ascended to be with God in Heaven after His crucifixion and resurrection, will return to earth and will be the judge of everyone who has ever lived.

In the past God overlooked such ignorance, but now he commands all people everywhere to repent.

For he has set a day when he will judge the world with justice by the man he has appointed. He has given proof of this to all men by raising him from the dead.

Acts 17:30,31

Jesus told a parable about that day of judgement. In it He contrasts the 'righteous' with the 'cursed'.

Then he will say to those on his left, 'Depart from me, you who are cursed, into the eternal fire prepared for the devil and his angels...'

Then they will go away to eternal punishment, but the righteous to eternal life.

Matthew 25:41,46

The 'righteous' are not the 'religious' but those who have chosen God's way to forgiveness. The 'cursed' are those facing God's punishment themselves because they have not allowed Jesus to do so.

The choice we face

This is the choice we face: the choice between the 'cursed' and the 'righteous'.

There is no middle ground. We will be viewed as 'cursed' if we have chosen not to receive God's forgiveness. That is how crucial it is to be counted among the 'righteous', by getting right with God, through receiving His forgiveness as we say 'yes' to Jesus.

The Way to Forgiveness and Reconciliation to God

We get right with God, and enjoy a relationship with Him, when we:

- acknowledge that we are in debt to God because of our sins
- acknowledge that Jesus paid that debt when He died on the cross to take our punishment
- repent of our sins, that is resolving not to continue in them
- ask God to forgive us
- choose to follow Jesus and live according to His teaching.

'...as we also have forgiven our debtors'

We return to that part of the Lord's Prayer which speaks of the need to have forgiven others as we ask God to forgive us.

Jesus was quick to expand on this. After finishing the prayer, He reinforced what God demands: God will not forgive our sins if we refuse to forgive those who have hurt us.

> *...But if you do not forgive men their sins, your Father will not forgive your sins.*
>
> Matthew 6:15

It is important to understand that Jesus was teaching this prayer, as a 'model' prayer, to those who would be followers of Jesus. Those followers, or disciples, would ultimately allow Jesus to be the one to pay their debts.

LUKE 6:27

Love for Enemies

27"But I tell you who hear me: Love mies, do good to those who hate you, 28 who curse you, pray for those who mis 29If someone strikes you on one cheek, t the other also. If someone takes your clo stop him from taking your tunic. Give fo

The great debt which each of us owes to God, for the accumulation of all our acts (and thoughts) which offend God, far exceeds the debts of others against us.

As we receive God's forgiveness, God expects that our gratitude for His mercy towards us should be reflected in our attitude towards others: an attitude of love and mercy rather than anger and a desire for revenge.

Jesus summed this up with a very simple instruction. Well, it is simple to understand though far from easy to observe!

...Love your enemies, do good to those who hate you, bless those who curse you, pray for those who ill-treat you.

Luke 6:27,28

The apostle Paul gave similar instructions to those who were followers of Jesus.

> *Get rid of all bitterness, rage and anger, brawling and slander, along with every form of malice...*
>
> Ephesians 4:31

> *...clothe yourselves with compassion, kindness, humility, gentleness and patience. Bear with each other and forgive whatever grievances you may have against one another.*
>
> *Forgive as the Lord forgave you.*
>
> Colossians 3:12-14

So it is very clear that God does not want us to be bitter or angry with others but to show kindness, love and compassion. Love and compassion should be our motive when forgiving others.

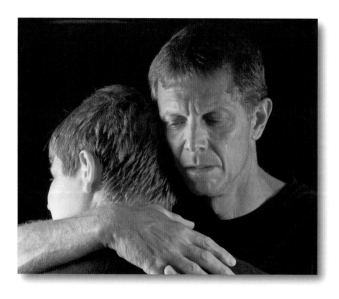

When we owe a debt to others

Of course, there will be times when we offend others, whether by our actions or by our words. That places us in the position of needing their forgiveness. Ultimately, the decision whether to forgive lies with the other person. However, we have the responsibility to do all we can to help that person to be able to forgive us.

The account of Zacchaeus, whose encounter with Jesus is recorded in Luke chapter 19, provides a good illustration of this.

Zacchaeus's Story

As a tax collector, Zacchaeus was despised by his fellow Jews. Tax collectors will never be the most popular of people. However, when they are corrupt (as Zacchaeus and others were), then a dislike of paying taxes can lead to a real hatred of those who collect them.

His attitude to his 'clients' was turned upside down - as indeed was his whole life - when he met with Jesus. The conversation between them is not recorded but what we do know is that Zacchaeus emerged as a changed man, promising that he would give half his wealth to the poor and would return four times the amounts he had taken unlawfully.

Zacchaeus wanted to demonstrate his remorse by making amends for the way he had treated the people in his community. No doubt he hoped that forgiveness - and reconciliation - would follow.

This is an example for us all: to apologise through our attitudes, words and actions, looking for ways of repairing the harm caused. In doing so, we will be trying to remove any barriers that prevent others from living peaceably with us.

The pain of guilt...

When one person offends against another, usually both parties suffer to some degree. There are occasions when the offender's suffering can be even greater because of the guilt he feels.

People who profess to follow the Bible's teaching (and know that God is willing to forgive sins) often say that their greatest difficulty is that they cannot forgive themselves. However, it is not unusual to find that the real difficulty is that the person has not truly confessed and truly repented.

If there has been no *genuine* sorrow or confession before God or perhaps no *genuine* wish to change their way of thinking or behaving, there will almost certainly be continued feelings of guilt, for they will not have received God's forgiveness.

God has promised to forgive our sins but we must acknowledge them and confess them.

If we claim to be without sin, we deceive ourselves and the truth is not in us. If we confess our sins, he is faithful and just and will forgive us our sins and purify us from all unrighteousness.
1 John 1:8,9

In the Bible the most notable confession of sin was by King David. An act of adultery with Bathsheba led to David being responsible for the death of her husband whom he set up to be killed in battle. David was overcome with guilt and depression until he finally confessed his sin and repented.

Then I acknowledged my sin to you and did not cover up my iniquity. I said, "I will confess my transgressions to the LORD " - and you forgave the guilt of my sin.

Psalm 32:5

... the joy of being forgiven

King David's actual confession is recorded in Psalm 51. This is a helpful psalm to use ourselves when we have sins to confess.

When David finally acknowledged his sin before God he experienced a great sense of joy:

Blessed is he whose transgressions are forgiven, whose sins are covered. Blessed is the man whose sin the LORD does not count against him and in whose spirit is no deceit.

Psalm 32:1,2

That same experience of joy and release can be ours too, when we confess our sins before God with true repentance.

Of course, there will be continued regret that we acted as we did. However, we can be confident that God will help us to fulfil all that He wants to do in our lives in the future, if we truly aim to please Him.

The Debt

Unforgiveness says:
'You owe me;
'You are in my debt;
'A debt so deep
'It can never be paid -
'I will not let you pay it.'

That debt is an iron chain
Which binds the injured to
the injurer;
The victim to the perpetrator;
The offended to the offender;
Growing old,
Bitter,
Imprisoned together.

Forgiveness
Is the choice to break that chain;
The courage to walk away,
The strength to say,
Despite the injury,
And the wrong,
'You owe me nothing'.

Here is true forgiveness:
That God
Angered by my rebellion;
My disobedience,
My waywardness,
Seeing the debt I owed to Him;
Seeing that I could not pay;
Came in His mercy,
Nailed all that I owed
To the cross of His Son,
Paid my debt Himself,
And spoke forgiveness over me.
I owe Him nothing.

And those cursed chains
That should have bound me
To His anger,
Become arms of love
That hold me
To His heart.
I owe Him everything.

Barbara J Parsons, 2010

38

What Next?

Many who have read this booklet will have done so because of a personal issue with forgiveness, either as one who has been hurt or as one who has hurt others.

If you are in either of those situations, I trust that you may have been encouraged and inspired (through the stories of others) to begin your own journey towards forgiveness.

Perhaps you are not yet ready to forgive others or perhaps you are finding it difficult to show remorse to people whom you have hurt and who cannot forgive you. Possibly you may be struggling with guilt, unable to forgive yourself.

Clearly, a booklet such as this will not provide answers to every question. If you do need personal help, please do seek out an appropriate friend, or perhaps a priest, pastor or counsellor, with whom you can explore further the steps which you need to take. Alternatively, you may wish to get one of the recommended books listed on page 40.

Forgiving others and accepting the forgiveness of others is so crucial to living peaceably and in harmony. Ultimately, however, God's forgiveness is our greatest need. It is our response now to God's offer of His forgiveness that determines our eternal destiny, on that day of final judgement, of the 'cursed' to eternal punishment and of the 'righteous' to eternal life.

If you would like to understand more about how to get right with God, I can recommend the website: www.crosscheck.org.uk. Alternatively, you may wish to contact BeaconLight Trust for a copy of the CrossCheck DVD.

John Phillips

Acknowledgements

We are very grateful to the following who have given permission for the use of the true stories of forgiveness featured in this booklet.

The Forgiveness Project: www.theforgivenessproject.com, for the stories of Mary Foley, Katy Hutchison and Ruth

David C. Cook, Colorado Springs, US and Eastbourne, UK. publishers of 'A Prison of My Own', Copyright © 2005 Diane Nichols

Plough Publishing House, Robertsbridge, publishers of 'Why Forgive?', Copyright © 2008 Johann Christoph Arnold

Authentic Media, Milton Keynes: www.authenticmedia.co.uk, publishers of 'Broken Wings', Copyright © 2006 Sheree Osborne

Bantam Press, London, publishers of 'The Damage Done', Copyright © 2008 Peter Woolf

Barry and Margaret Mizen, who have set up The Jimmy Mizen Foundation: www.jimmymizen.org
Nationwide Christian Trust: www.nationwidechristiantrust.com, publishers of the DVD, 'The Jimmy Mizen Story'

Ray and Vi Donovan, who can be contacted through Forgiveness Ministries: www.forgivenessministries.org.

We are grateful, too, for permission to use the poem from 'Seeds of Forgiveness', © 2009 BAR NONE Books and the author.

Recommended Books

Why Forgive?, by Johann Christoph Arnold,
      published by Plough Publishing House, 2008

True Forgiveness, by RT Kendall,
      published by Hodder & Stoughton, 2001

How to Forgive ... When You Don't Feel Like It, by June Hunt,
      published by Harvest House Publishers, 2007